# 52 Ways to Teach Children to Pray

## Easy-to-do Activities for Ages 3 -12

**Editor** ................................................................*Crystal Abell*

**Illustrator** .............................................................*Fran Kizer*

Copyright © 2003 • Twelfth Printing
Rainbow Publishers • P.O. Box 261129 • San Diego, CA 92196
www.rainbowpublishers.com

RB36105
ISBN 0-937282-62-6
church and ministry/ministry resources/children's ministry

Give ear to my words, O LORD,
consider my meditation.
Hearken unto the voice of my cry,
my King, and my God:
for unto Thee will I pray.
*Psalm 5:1-2*

**52**

**Ways to Teach Children to Pray**

Easy-to-do Activities for Ages 3-12

# Introduction

Prayer is talking to God — telling Him our needs, expressing thanks, confessing wrongs, and interceding for others — and listening for His response. Prayer is also worship — expressing our love to the Lord for all He is and all He does. To put it simply, prayer is communication. Children know how to talk with others, so if they have a desire to communicate with God as well, they need only to take a step in that direction. For this reason, the task facing the children's leaders at church is to encourage boys and girls to want to communicate with God.

Learning to pray is a lifelong journey, and the natural faith of a child gives him a head start. If we can help children develop sound attitudes and teach them basic truths about God and prayer, we can guide them in growing into mature Christians.

We need to help boys and girls become aware of God's loving presence and encourage them in expressing their appreciation and gratitude to Him. Then as they grow, children will see that prayer involves total response — submission of one's will and way to God's perfect will and way.

The activities in this book are an effort to stimulate this type of prayer response in children. The crafts, games, puzzles, discussion guides, and other classroom activities will help boys and girls realize that there are many kinds of prayers and many ways of praying. Students will learn about prayers of confession, prayers of intercession, prayers of thanksgiving, and prayers of praise. And they will learn how to pray for others as well as for themselves.

Children will come face-to-face with proper attitudes about both God and prayer. In addition to perceiving God as a loving Heavenly Father who wants us to talk to Him, your students will learn that God is always near and that He is strong, good, and wise. They will understand that God always answers our prayers as He sees fit because He loves us and knows what is best for us.

In short, the 52 activities that follow will provide many ways to help children learn that God ALWAYS listens, ALWAYS cares, and ALWAYS answers. We need only to open our hearts and minds before Him.

## 52 Ways to Teach Children to Pray

### — Easy-to-do Activities for Ages 3 -12 —

## CONTENTS

# 1 Thanks Banks

OBJECTIVE: To teach children in a tangible way to thank God for His intervention in their lives

*Appropriate for ages 6 to 9*

Many parents use an allowance to reward their children for work done around the house; the allowance can be tangible evidence to the child that his work is appreciated. Similarly, God appreciates our remembrance of Him for what He does in our lives, and giving thanks can be more consistent if we have a visual symbol to remind us to do so.

Help the children in your class create "Thanks Banks" to aid them in developing an "attitude of gratitude." First introduce how they are to use the banks by explaining:

"The Bible says 'O give thanks unto the LORD; call upon His name: make known His deeds among the people' (Psalm 105:1). Let's do just what this Bible verse tells us to do. Each day we can keep track of the times we remember to 'give thanks unto the Lord,' and next week we will 'make known His deeds' by sharing with each other the things He has done for us."

It may be helpful to have a completed bank to show as an example to the children before they begin working on their own.

Ask the congregation in advance to provide cardboard cylinders from paper towels or wrapping paper. Cut the cylinders into three-inch tubes. Help the children tape construction paper coverings over both ends of their tubes and cut a small slit at least 1" long in one end of the bank. Instruct them to write "Thanks Bank" on the tube and to decorate it with colorful stickers which you provide.

Next supply each child with several pieces of plain white paper about 1 by 2 inches. Have the children write the words "Thank you, God" on each one. These will be the "deposit slips."

Using your sample craft, say to the children,

I THANKED GOD THIS WEEK FOR KEEPING US SAFE DURING THE BIG STORM.

"Each time you remember to thank God during the week, you may put a 'Thank You, God' deposit slip into your Thanks Bank. On the back of the slip, write down what you are thanking God for so that you can tell the class next week. Remember to bring your Thanks Banks next week so we can all share with each other what God has done."

Be sure to schedule the sharing time in your plans for the next class period. To get the slips out of the banks, the children may simply cut a hole through the construction paper at one end and shake the slips out.

If your students seem to enjoy the project, you may want to plan a block of time for sharing every week. Remember to provide new sheets of construction paper to replace the end covers and retape them over the tubes.

# 2 | Genuine Prayer

OBJECTIVE: To discuss with children the idea that it is natural to pray

*Appropriate for ages 6 to 12*

Since prayer is communication with God, we should not let it become mechanical, or an act of merely saying words. Discuss this with your class, making sure to emphasize that prayer is a natural conversation.

To help encourage communicative prayer, suggest some things to pray for. As you talk about the following list, ask the children what they feel some of the prayers could include. Encourage the students to add to the list any other ideas that they can think of.

We can pray:

- For special guidance from the Lord.
- For our loved ones and friends, mentioning them by name.
- For missionaries and their individual needs.
- To confess our sins.
- For those in authority over us.
- With thanksgiving, identifying the things we are thankful for.
- For those who need to know Christ.
- For the sick and afflicted.
- To ask for help with our own spiritual needs.

- For the people we have trouble getting along with.
- For the church and individual believers.

# 3 Rebus Prayer Poems

OBJECTIVE: To help young children express their love to God using visual symbols

*Appropriate for ages 4 to 6*

For children who are beginning readers, the use of rebus charts can make learning fun and effective. To make a rebus chart use descriptive pictures in place of some of the words in a prayer. For example, use pictures for the words in parentheses in this prayer:

We thank You, God, for daily (bread)
   For (apples) and (cherries) red;
For (milk) and (ice cream), special treats,
   For all the things so good to eat;
For (cheese) and (meat) that makes us strong,
   We thank You, God, the whole day long.

Read the words to the children, slowly and rhythmically, while pointing to the pictures. Let the children say the words that the pictures represent. By the time you repeat the prayer poem several times the children will be familiar with it; when they see these food items at home they will be encouraged to repeat the prayer.

As a creative project for your class, you may write more prayer poems and let the children add the pictures. Write out the new poem on a piece of paper, leaving a good amount of space for the pictures. Duplicate the poem and pass out the sheet to each child. As before, read the poem slowly to the class; when you come to the blank spots, ask the children what they think should be put in. When they guess an appropriate word, direct the students to draw it in the open space. Keep these symbols fairly simple so the children will be able to recognize and draw them easily.

Another way to let the students add the rebus symbols is for you to cut out the pictures ahead of time from magazines, newspapers and left-over

Dear God, you made the ☀ so bright, The ☽ and ✨✨ to shine at night, The pretty 🌷🌷🌷 and the 🌳🌳 so tall; We thank you that You made them all.

teaching aids or take-home papers. Although this may be time-consuming if your class size is rather large, the children will enjoy having realistic pictures for their poems.

Yet another option is to purchase a variety of stickers. Children love to make sticker books, and what better contents could they have than a collection of thanksgiving and praise for the God Who loves them?

To take this idea further, let the children themselves "write" the poem by suggesting what they would like to pray about. They might want to do a poem about their families, or about nature, etc. Use a poster board to write down their ideas and let them take turns coming forward to draw the symbol.

# 4 Pray When The Need Arises

OBJECTIVE: To help children see that we can pray whenever we need to

*Appropriate for ages 3 to 6*

Discuss with young children the idea that we can pray whenever the need arises, wherever we are. The Lord is always ready to hear and answer. We don't have to wait for a specific hour such as when we get up in the morning, when we go to bed at night, or before we eat a meal . . . and we don't have to wait until we get to church on Sunday morning. God is ALWAYS available, He ALWAYS hears and He ALWAYS answers.

Biblical illustrations to use in your lesson are as follows:

a. Paul and Silas prayed in prison. (Acts 16:25-40).

b. Hannah prayed in the temple. (I Samuel 1:1-18)

c. Nehemiah prayed day and night before going to the king. (Nehemiah 1)

---

# 5 Prayer Maze

OBJECTIVE: To help children realize the need to watch for things that get in the way of prayer time

*Appropriate for ages 7 to 10*

Duplicate the puzzle on page 11 for each child. As the students try to find their way through the maze, they will run into "dead-ends" that represent obstacles to prayer. Ask what they think they can do to avoid these obstacles. For example, if we have an unforgiving attitude, we must go to the person(s) involved and offer forgiveness. If we are too tired to pray, perhaps it is a sign that we need to plan our time better or that the time of day we are setting aside for prayer is not the best for us.

Emphasize to your class that no matter what the reason, we can ask God to give us the desire for true communication with Him. He can motivate us to change our poor attitudes or the circumstances that may be holding us back. Before class is over, pray with your students.

# Prayer Maze

Find your way through the maze to the Bible verse at the end. Watch out for the hindrances along the way — they'll get you nowhere! Can you think of any other obstacles to prayer that we should watch out for?

# 6 Beginner's Grace

OBJECTIVE: To provide real experience in thanking God for our food

*Appropriate for ages 3 to 6*

When young children have an opportunity to prepare, serve and taste real food, then thanking God for His provision can become a genuine, heart-felt response of love and gratitude. To help teach your younger students about table prayers, provide a first-hand experience.

You will need a toaster, bread, butter or margarine, several knives and a shaker of sugar and cinnamon. Also provide napkins and small paper plates.

Choose volunteers to complete the various stages of preparing the cinnamon toast; try to involve every child in some capacity. At least two students can take charge of the actual toasting. They will need close adult supervision to help prevent any mishaps. Several more children will spread on the margarine after the bread is toasted. The next group of helpers will shake on the cinnamon and sugar mixture. You may want to help them do the first few slices so that they can see how much to sprinkle on.

Two or three children may be the servers. If you wish to provide something to drink, it would probably be best to pour the drink into small paper cups ahead of time and let the children set these down at the table one at a time. Make sure each child has a napkin!

Before the children eat, have them offer a prayer of thanksgiving to God for the good-tasting toast. Explain to them that we should always thank God for what He provides for us. He made the grain that grows in the fields, and He gave people the creativity to harvest the grain and make it into bread.

The children may already be familiar with the

following traditional prayer. You may choose to use this prayer alone or to use it as a starting point for the children to move on to thank God in their own way for His provision.

> God is great,
>   God is good;
> Let us thank Him
>   For our food.
>
> By His hands
>   We all are fed;
> Thank You, Lord,
>   For daily bread.
>
> Amen.

# 7 Praying Bible People

OBJECTIVE: To learn through research method about Bible people who have effectively prayed

*Appropriate for ages 9 to 12*

How can we be sure that when we pray, God cares and actually listens to us? The examples of many people in the Bible are strong indicators that God has listened in the past and therefore will listen to us today.

Invite your juniors to take part in a small research project to discover who some of these people are and what they prayed. Each Sunday ask a different student to be ready the following week to tell or read about a Bible person who prayed effectively.

If your church has a library or resource center, try to find books written on a younger level that pertain to the Bible passages listed on this page. If these are not available, you may want to do some initial research on your own with a Bible commentary and write down on 3 by 5 inch cards any information that would be helpful to the students. Try as much as possible to "translate" the commentaries into words your juniors can understand, but be careful not to take away the challenge of the project. Offer these cards to the students after they select the prayers on which they want to work.

Another possible resource could be your pastor. Ask him beforehand if he would be willing to help the children with their research projects, and give him the list of passages so that he has time to gather his own materials first. If he is available, invite him to come to your class on the day you introduce the project so that he can tell the children himself that he is ready to help them. This may encourage the students who might otherwise be shy to approach him later when they are working on the project. It will also be an excellent opportunity for your pastor and the children to get better acquainted with each other.

As an extra incentive, try to locate any "Bible-times" costumes your church may have left over from Christmas pageants or plays. On the student's day to share with the class about his findings, let him wear the costume and perhaps present the report in "first person."

Prayer will become more meaningful as the children respond with the Scripture readings and reports they choose. This project can also help make the lessons more interesting and memorable as the young people share responsibility for making them successful.

The following are references for some of the notable prayers recorded in the Bible:

- Genesis 18:22-33—Abraham prays for Sodom to be spared
- II Samuel 7:18-29—David prays when denied the privilege of building the temple
- I Kings 3:5-14—Solomon asks God for wisdom
- I Kings 8:22-30—Solomon dedicates the temple
- Daniel 9:15-19—Daniel prays for the captive Jews
- Habakkuk 3:11-19—Habakkuk prays for deliverance
- Matthew 6:9-13—The Lord's Prayer
- John 17:1-26—Christ's intercessory prayer
- Ephesians 3:14-21—Paul's prayer for the Ephesians

# 8 Litanies

*Appropriate for ages 9 to 12*

A litany is a responsive prayer in which one person makes supplication before God or praises Him for something and the rest of the group responds in agreement. Psalm 136 is an example of a litany. The phrase "for His mercy endureth for ever" is the group's response.

Your class can write worshipful litanies in response to a variety of questions, such as "What do you like best about our church?" or "How does God help you day by day?" Each question becomes a theme for a litany, with each student giving an answer to the question and the rest of the class responding with a common phrase.

Let the class choose a theme (praise, thanksgiving, or requests, etc.) and give suggestions for the things they want to say. Choose a response which contains the major idea of your theme, such as, "We give You thanks, O Lord," or "We ask You to help us, O God," or "Lord of all, we praise Your name."

When the litany is completed, let a different child read each of the theme sentences to which the group responds together. A sample follows of how your class might create a litany of thanks:

Student 1: "We are glad that it is now warm enough for us to play outside after school."
Group: "Thank You, Jesus."
Student 2: "We are thankful for our friends and the fun we can have together."
Group: "Thank You, Jesus."
Student 3: "We are very grateful for our homes and for our families who love us so much."
Group: "Thank You, Jesus."
Student 4: "O Lord, we are so glad You love us all the time."
Group: "Thank You, Jesus."
All: "Amen."

# 9 Prayer For Absentees

OBJECTIVE: To remind children to pray for their peers and to encourage those who are absent

*Appropriate for ages 5 to 10*

"Out of sight, out of mind" does not have to be true for your classroom! Show concern for absentees while teaching your students to pray for others.

Provide a sheet of construction paper and some crayons or markers for each student. Direct the children to write their names in large letters in the middle of their papers (for the younger ones you may need to do this for them ahead of class time). Once they have written their names, the boys and girls may draw whatever they like on the paper. Encourage them to draw things that they are interested in (baseball cards, mystery books, etc.) or things that they like to do, such as playing the piano, skateboarding, and so on. Tell them that this will be their very own name card, so whatever they choose to draw is acceptable.

To use the name cards, you should have a chair set up in the classroom for every student every week, whether he is present or not. As soon as the class has assembled, ask your students if anyone is absent. Keep your roll book handy to catch the names of any pupils that your class doesn't remember.

If a child is absent, place his name card on an empty chair. Ask if anyone knows why he is not present (for example, he may be ill or on a trip). Then allow time for the children to pray for their peers by name. Children who have a tendency toward shyness or who show a lack of confidence in praying publicly may be willing to pray for a specific absentee if that student is a personal friend. For this reason, you may want to ask for volunteers to pray for individuals of their own choice.

Children are impressed by interest shown when they are absent. Sending a little postcard

through the mail would not only help your students express in a more tangible way their concern, but it would also encourage your absentees. At the end of each class period, provide enough 4 by 6 inch cards to cover each absentee. On one side either write yourself or have the children write something like "We prayed for you during class. We hope to see you next time." Then let the students write words of encouragement and sign their names. Use your roll book to get the absentee's address and use the name of your class in the return address.

As your students begin to see that their teacher and peers care about them, they will want to express similar thoughtfulness toward others. As a result, the prayer time in your classroom can become very meaningful to your students.

# 10 Apostle Paul

OBJECTIVE: To promote the idea of prayer as a part of one's lifestyle

*Appropriate for ages 9 to 12*

Lessons from various scriptural examples can show the children in your class that biblical people have prayed in a number of situations. The boys and girls need to understand, however, that prayer is not just something that these people relied upon once in a while in the face of troubled times; prayer for most of these people was a natural part of their lifestyles.

To help your students share this perspective, challenge the boys and girls in your class to spend time during the week pretending to be the Apostle Paul.

Duplicate the Scripture references and "thought questions" on page 17 for the students to use. Through the study of these Scripture references the children will learn about Paul's prayer life. Tell the children to go into a quiet room at home with their Bible, a pencil and the study sheet. As they read the Word and write down their thoughts, the children should try to think of songs of comfort and peace or of praise and thanksgiving that Paul might have sung if he had known them. At the close of their worship time, the students may write a short prayer expressing their thoughts and feelings to God.

The following week, encourage the boys and girls to share their written thoughts with the rest of the class. Suggest that they lead the class in singing the songs as well. Then discuss the idea of prayer as a part of one's lifestyle, asking the children to name ways that they can make prayer meaningful in their own lives as Paul did. Close with a time of silent prayer.

# Apostle Paul Worksheet

Use the following Scripture references to read about the apostle Paul:
Acts 16:25-40 — Paul and Silas sing while they are in jail, then an earthquake hits;
Acts 17:16-31 — Paul speaks before the philosophers of Athens;
Acts 27:13-44 — Paul is shipwrecked after a severe storm at sea.

Now think about these questions and write down some of your thoughts:
A. What would make you want to sing if you were chained and in prison? _____
_____
B. What kinds of "prisons" are there for us? (We can be imprisoned by bad attitudes, alcohol, broken homes, etc.) _____
_____
C. How can God help us escape these prisons? _____
_____
D. How can you witness about your faith in God, like Paul did in Athens? What would you say?
_____
E. Are there times when the "storms of life" frighten you? How can you know that God will keep you safe? _____
_____

---

# 11 Special Prayers Crossword

OBJECTIVE: To help children learn from biblical examples to pray in any life situation

*Appropriate for ages 9 to 12*

What does the average child pray about? More than likely he prays for his parents and other relatives, for his pets, for the weather, etc. The stories told in the Bible represent many different situations lived out by many different people, some with positive outcomes and some with negative results. As the children in your class work this crossword, they will be able to see how often people turned to God in prayer.

Duplicate the puzzle on page 18 for each child. The students will need to have a Bible to look up the Scriptures to learn the crossword answers. When the pupils finish, begin discussing with them what kinds of situations they can pray for, such as motivation to study for a big test or strength to treat an unfriendly schoolmate with kindness. End the session with prayer.

Answers are on page 64.

# Special Prayers Crossword

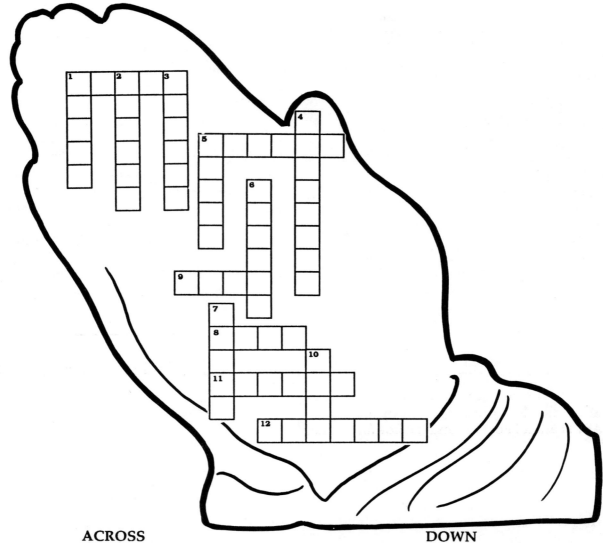

### ACROSS

1. He prayed while His friends slept. (Matthew 26:36-40)
5. He prayed and gave thanks even though it meant death. (Daniel 6:7-10)
8. A returned exile, he prayed about the guilt of the people in marrying foreigners. (Ezra 10:1-5)
9. She prayed and gave thanks to God for being able to live long enough to see Baby Jesus. (Luke 2:36-39)
11. He prayed for God's help in a contest with the priests of Baal. (I Kings 18:36-39)
12. He prayed to dedicate the temple. (I Kings 8:22)

### DOWN

1. He prayed from the belly of the fish. (Jonah 2:1)
2. He prayed for guidance in choosing a king. (I Samuel 8:6)
3. He prayed for his great strength to return. (Judges 16:28)
4. This dying king prayed, and Isaiah brought God's word that he would live fifteen years longer. (Isaiah 38:2-5)
5. He prayed for his dying son. (II Samuel 12:15-17)
6. She prayed for a son. (I Samuel 1:9-11)
7. He prayed by the body of Dorcas and she opened her eyes. (Acts 9:36, 40)
10. He gave thanks while facing a shipwreck. (Acts 27:30-35)

# 12 Thankful Book

OBJECTIVE: To make a craft that reminds students to show their gratitude to God

*Appropriate for ages 6 to 9*

Sometimes we show a natural human tendency to take for granted the goodness in our lives. Children can do this too, for they were given virtually everything they have had since they can remember. To help the children in your class develop an attitude of thankfulness for the people, places, and things that God has brought into their lives, help them make a scrapbook representing these things.

Provide each student with several pieces of plain white paper for the inside pages of their scrapbooks. The children can use photographs, drawings, and pictures cut from magazines to glue or tape on each page. Following each illustration, the boys and girls may write captions or notes describing why they are thankful for the people, places, and things pictured and what they learn about God through them. Tell the students to keep a few blank pages so that they can add to the book later if desired.

Hand out to each child two sheets of construction paper for the front and back covers. The students should write a title on the front such as "I Am Thankful For . . . " and include an "author

line" for their names underneath. Either staple the pages together or punch holes along the left edge and let the children tie the book together with pieces of colorful yarn.

# 13 Sing-A-Prayer

OBJECTIVE: To allow younger children to create their own songs about prayer

*Appropriate for ages 4 to 8*

Discuss with your young students the concept that we don't always have to kneel, close our eyes, and fold our hands when we pray. The main reason we do these things is so that we won't be distracted by watching other people. God wants us to focus on Him when we pray. It does not matter to God what we talk to Him about, as long as we remember that He wants to hear what is truly in our thoughts.

Children like to sing little tunes and they learn them easily, so it would be natural to encourage them to just put their thoughts about Jesus and God into a song. You can use simple, familiar tunes but change the words to create prayer songs for your class to sing together. For example:

(Tune: Mary Had A Little Lamb)
Thank you, God, for loving me,
  Loving me, loving me.
Thank you, God, for loving me,
  I will love You too.

(Tune: The Farmer In The Dell)
God gives us rain and sun,
  And pretty flowers that grow,
Friends and family and lots of fun,
  Oh, how I love Him so.

(Tune: London Bridge)
Jesus died for you and me,
  You and me, you and me.
Jesus died for you and me;
  That's why He's our Savior.

To gradually broaden the repertoire of your class, encourage the children to suggest words for new prayer songs every few months. The songs can cover a variety of topics, ranging from thankfulness for God's gifts to petitions for particular needs. Even if the children choose the same tunes, which is probable since they like repetition, the experience should be beneficial for them. They will enjoy the opportunity to be creative, and their involvement will help boost self-confidence. The songs can become a regular part of your lesson plans to use for prayer time or songtime. More importantly, though, the children will begin singing them on their own outside the classroom setting.

# 14 Praying God's Word

OBJECTIVE: To become aware of God's guidance by making His Word a part of prayer

*Appropriate for ages 9 to 12 (and the entire congregation)*

In Mark 12:24, Jesus said to the Sadducees, "Are you not in error because you do not know the Scriptures or the power of God?" (NIV). Becoming familiar with the Scriptures is much more than a show of knowledge. Through the Bible we receive direction for living in the best possible manner. Psalm 16:11 says God will show us the path of life. With such a wealth of information available to us, it seems only natural to use the promises from the Bible in our own prayer life.

To use this idea with your students, let them first choose a Scripture promise to work with. Direct them to read the verse aloud and then to pray it back to God in their own words. For example:

Read: "I will instruct thee and teach thee in the way which thou shalt go: I will guide thee with Mine eye." (Psalm 32:8)

Pray: "Lord, You promise to teach me which direction I should go, now and in the future. Thank You for guiding me."

The following references are just a few of the promises your class may use:

Psalm 37:3-6
I Corinthians 10:13
Psalm 6:9
Isaiah 40:29-31

Joshua 1:9
James 4:8a
John 16:33
Matthew 28:20b
Exodus 14:14

# 15 Prayer Basics

OBJECTIVE: To discuss with your students basic understandings about prayer

*Appropriate for ages 9 to 12 (and the entire congregation)*

Prayer is a very personal relationship between an individual and God. When we pray, we are presenting ourselves before Someone Who is all powerful and yet at the same time is personal enough that we can call Him our Friend.

Do the children in your class know what prayer is? Do they understand the reasons we have for talking with God? Do they know how to pray?

Read through the following discourse, then use it as a guideline to help explain to your students the what, why, how, where, and when of prayer. As you introduce each topic, try to open up discussion so that you can get an idea of what your pupils already understand, then build upon that. Reserve some time at the end of the discussion for the children to pray on their own.

**What Is Prayer?** When we ask this question, the responses are varied. Prayer may be defined as talking with God, usually as a part of a loving relationship with Him. Prayer may be a petition for God's help or the expression of our needs or gratitude.

What then is prayer? It is communicating with God in silent or spoken words, in verbal, written or musical expression. Prayer is simply talking to God. It is telling God about our joys and sorrows. It is telling Him about our problems and needs. Just as we go to visit a friend and talk with him freely, prayer is visiting God.

**Why Do We Pray?** An important reason for praying is to confess our sins, to tell God we are sorry for any wrongdoing. Sin is not just the acts of wrong for which we are punished in society, such as stealing and murder. Sin also comes from having negative attitudes, bearing a grudge, gossip, and so on. Sin is anything we say or do that is against the will of God.

I John 1:9 says "If we confess our sins, He is faithful and just to forgive us our sins, and to cleanse us from all unrighteousness." God wants us to be truthful with Him, to come to Him when we have done wrong. Then He can offer forgiveness for our sins and we can forget them as if they never happened.

A second reason for praying is to offer thanksgiving to God. Every day we can thank the Lord for something in our lives. The list of things for which we can be thankful would be too long to write, but it could include something as general as a pretty day to something specific such as the way a particular problem has worked out.

Many times we pray seeking help and blessings from the Lord. These are called petitionary prayers, the kind where we make a request to God. We believe that God is willing to hear these requests and that as His children, we have the opportunity to ask Him for both material and spiritual blessings. Isaiah 65:24 says, "It shall come to pass, that before they call, I will answer; and while they are yet speaking, I will hear."

We must learn to consider our needs and desires in accordance with God's will. We should ask ourselves, "Is this a real need? Is it loving and honest?" Then we must have faith that God will answer our prayer.

A fourth reason for praying is to ask for help or blessings for someone else. This is called a prayer of intercession. Our concern for others causes us to try to understand their needs and to take them to the Lord.

Another reason for praying is to show our love and appreciation to God. This is a prayer of adoration. In this prayer one forgets himself and all others. He simply stands in awe at the majesty of God.

**How Do We Pray?** Sometimes it is helpful to precede our prayer time with the reading of a devotional book or a portion of the Bible. This can help to put us in a worshipful attitude.

To refresh our memory of the people and situations for whom we are praying, it is a good idea to keep a prayer list and to look it over before we pray. This way we can be specific when we bring those needs before God.

There is no special form to use in prayer. We usually begin by addressing the Lord and end by saying "Amen," which means "so be it." Whatever we say in between is up to us. Jesus gave us the Lord's Prayer as our model; it reminds us to acknowledge the Lordship of God, to seek His will, to give thanks, to confess our sins, and to ask for His help in our daily lives. If we keep the Lord's Prayer in mind, we can use it as our example.

Sometimes we kneel when we pray to show our respect to God, but we do not always have to get down on our knees. God will still hear us if we are standing up or lying down, if our eyes are open or closed, if we pray out loud or quietly. It does not matter how we pray, as long as we talk with God sincerely.

**Where Do We Pray?** Certainly we pray in church, but the other places we pray depend upon each of us individually. We can pray while doing dishes and dusting the furniture. We can

pray while riding the bus to school. We can pray while taking a walk through the park. We can pray at any location, and God will hear us.

**When Should We Pray?** Some people like to pray in the morning because they feel this starts their day better. Others prefer to pray in the evening when they may feel they have more time. There may be many times during the day when we offer short prayers to God. It is not important when we pray, but that we set aside some time for talking with God each day. Psalm 55:17 says, "Evening, and morning, and at noon, will I pray, and cry aloud: and He shall hear my voice."

We can pray at any time. God will always listen to our prayers, no matter when or where or how or why we feel like talking to Him.

# 16 Lord's Prayer Chain

OBJECTIVE: To enable children to describe the Lord's Prayer in their own words

*Appropriate for ages 6 to 11*

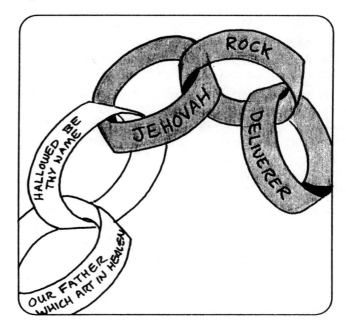

Trying to understand something as the sum of its parts usually offers a better learning process than tackling the whole concept at once. The same can be true for teaching children about the Lord's Prayer (Matthew 6:9-15). Children love to make paper chains, so use this activity to help the students come up with their own interpretation of the Lord's Prayer.

Cut a dozen or so strips of colored construction paper about 1 by 9 inches. Use one color for the various phrases of the Lord's Prayer. You can either print the phrases ahead of time or let the children do this during class. Also cut about two dozen strips of construction paper using another color for the descriptions of the phrases.

Begin the class project with the first strip(s), which should say, "Our Father Which art in heaven, Hallowed be Thy Name." Ask the children to share all the names they can think of that are used in the Bible to refer to God. Direct the pupils to print these names on the contrasting-colored strips. Attach these together with tape or glue, looping each through the previous strip to make a chain.

Next, attach to the chain the strip(s) with the second phrase of the Lord's Prayer ("Thy kingdom come. Thy will be done in earth, as it is in heaven"). Now let the children prepare paper strips with their ideas of what God's kingdom is. Guide the discussion by asking "Where should God reign?" Possible answers would be in our lives, our families, our nation, etc.

The next phrase to put on a strip is "Give us this day our daily bread." The children can make strips showing some of what we need as we live on this earth, such as food, houses, and clothing. Help the students understand that God already knows what we need before we ask, but it is still important to ask in order to show Him our faith and dependence.

The next slip will read "And forgive us our debts, as we forgive our debtors." Help the children see that these "debts" are not financial obligations but sins against God and man. This phrase is to teach us to not only ask for forgiveness,

but also to grant it generously to others. The children can make strips for some of the things that could be considered "debts."

"And lead us not into temptation, but deliver us from evil," is the next major link. This is a plea for strength and protection from Satan's attacks. Direct the children to look up Ephesians 6:10-18 to find out about God's armor and write down these armor items.

The last major link will be "For Thine is the kingdom, and the power, and the glory, for ever. Amen." God can set up His *Kingdom* in us by our giving Him total reign over our bodies, our minds, our talents, our time, etc. He has *power* over everything which He often demonstrates through miracles, and He gives us power to be strong and to do His will. We can give God the *glory* He deserves by praying, singing praises to Him, and living according to His will.

As a reminder of what the Lord's Prayer means to us today, hang the chain across the room when it is completed. This project can also be extended over several weeks by working on only one phrase each week, which would allow more time for discussion of the various aspects of the Lord's Prayer.

# 17 ( Pass-It-On-Prayer )

OBJECTIVE: To boost children's confidence in praying out loud

*Appropriate for ages 4 to 12*

When you ask for a volunteer to pray out loud for the rest of the class, you may notice that not all of the boys and girls raise their hands. The reason is probably not a lack of openness to the idea; some children may simply be too shy or afraid to pray out loud. While praying aloud is not absolutely essential to the Christian lifestyle, its benefits to the individual are worth the possible discomfort in overcoming the fear. Vocalizing our thoughts helps us to communicate them better, and we believe what we say when we say what we believe.

To help the children in your class gain assurance and ease in praying out loud, introduce the concept of a "pass-it-on" prayer. With this idea your students will have the opportunity to say one or two sentences and then pass the prayer along. The next child may either continue with the thoughts from the previous student or pray about something else, and the last student can end the prayer.

At prayer time, gather the students into a circle. To begin, either select a child who is usually willing to pray or ask for a volunteer. In a class of younger children, it would be best for the teacher to begin the prayer and then let the children follow with their thoughts. Having a theme

for your prayer time, such as things to thank God for, can be effective in stimulating participation. If you have several children in your class who are hesitant, you may want to approach the whole idea as a voluntary prayer time. Then after your children are used to the concept, start going around the entire circle. Be careful not to push those who are still not ready.

25

# 18 Outdoor Prayer And Worship Time

OBJECTIVE: To offer a sensory experience with nature that encourages thankfulness

*Appropriate for ages 3 to 11*

Children as well as adults sense the nearness and greatness of God as they behold the beauties of nature and God's creation. There seems to be no better place to praise God for His wonderful goodness to us than while we are outdoors, surrounded by the trees, the flowers and the sky. Prayers of thanksgiving for God's provision may become more real to the children if they can actually be surrounded by ripe fruits or grains. By using the various senses — touching the grass, seeing the fluffy clouds, hearing the birds sing, tasting the fruit, smelling the flowers, etc. — children will long remember this learning experience.

Even if your church is not located near the countryside, using a park or even your church lawn can provide the opportunity to worship God while exploring nature. Once you arrive at the site chosen, gather the children in a circle and begin to focus their attention on their surroundings. Together, look at the sky and praise the Lord for the glorious heavens He created for us to enjoy. If it is cloudy, ask the children what kinds of shapes or animals they can imagine in the clouds. Talk about the grass and thank God for the green carpet He has provided on which to play and sit. (You may wish to allow the students to take off their shoes and feel the cool grass between their toes.) Let them touch the trees and try to describe what the bark feels like. Tell them to count how many different smells come from the variety of flowers. Try to see who can come closest to imitating the sounds made by the birds.

Ask the children to name ways in which God has provided for our needs through nature. If your schedule allows for snack time, bring a basketful of fruit and let the children choose what they would like to eat. Bring as wide a variety as

possible, including some less common fruits (for instance kiwi, plums, or persimmons) and discuss with the children how creative God was when He made so many different kinds of fruits. If this activity is not possible, use the example of grapes turning into raisins when they are dried in the sun to illustrate how God designed the aspects of nature to continually interact together.

Emphasize to the children that even with all the beauty of nature, one part of God's creation is more precious than everything else: the people. And because He loves us so much, God chooses to communicate with us through prayer. Unlike the blue jays, dandelions, and oak trees, we are the only part of creation that can talk to God.

Direct the children to offer a prayer of thanksgiving and praise to God. If you wish, sing the hymn "This is My Father's World" before heading back into the classroom.

26

# 19 Prayer Murals

OBJECTIVE: To creatively remind your students that we can pray anytime and anywhere

*Appropriate for ages 6 to 12*

Mount a long piece of paper on a wall in your classroom (butcher paper is probably best, but if this is not available you might use white shelf paper or try using the back side of discarded computer paper). Perhaps you could glue or draw at the center of the mural a large silhouette of a boy and girl bowing their heads in prayer.

Discuss with the children in your class what kinds of pictures they could draw together which would show all the times and places they can pray. After each child has decided what he wants to draw, give out crayons or colored chalk (markers might bleed through to the wall) and let the students draw.

When the children have completed the mural, give them a chance to describe what they have drawn, then end the session with prayer.

# 20 A Prayer Pledge

OBJECTIVE: To foster an attitude of reverence at prayer time

*Appropriate for ages 6 to 12*

For a junior class that shows a tendency to have difficulty in quieting down, a prayer pledge may be helpful. The pledge can serve to help create an atmosphere of respect and to prepare the class for prayer time. If solemnly and seriously repeated after the teacher, the pledge should have a definite effect on the students' attitudes during prayer.

You may allow class time for your students to write a pledge of their own, or use the one provided:

"I will try to the best of my ability to keep an attitude of reverence at all times during prayer; to bow my head, to close my eyes, and to listen attentively when others are praying."

Use the pledge often as a reminder to your class to be reverent.

# 21 Pharisees And Publicans

OBJECTIVE: To recognize the proper attitudes for prayer

*Appropriate for age 6 to teens*

As your students begin to see that we can pray anytime and anywhere for anything, start paying attention to their attitudes. Do the children correctly feel that God is their Friend, that they can be themselves with Him? Or do they perhaps think that they need to put their best foot forward, to somehow impress God and the people around them?

Jesus told a parable about a religious leader and a tax collector to illustrate the proper attitudes we should have. Use this story in the same way with your class.

First, read Luke 18:9-14 and briefly tell the story of the Pharisee and the publican. Then discuss the meaning of the parable by asking your students the following questions:

"What was the Temple?" (Where the people worshipped God)

"What was the Pharisee's attitude?" (He was proud, he told God how good and important he was, he did not praise God)

"What was the publican's attitude?" (He knew he had done wrong and asked God to forgive him, he was humble before the Lord)

"What is the difference between someone who prays just to show off or sound good and one who prays because he loves God and wants to talk to Him?" (The first person focuses on himself and tries to get attention from other people, the second really believes what he is praying and listens for God to respond)

What kind of attitude does the Lord want us to have when we pray? (Sincere, humble, respectful, trusting in Him)

Following the discussion, provide 12 by 18 inch construction paper for the children to make posters illustrating prayerful attitudes. Direct them to write at the top: "Every one that exalteth himself shall be abased; and he that humbleth himself shall be exalted." (Luke 18:14) Underneath the verse the children should draw a thick line down the center to separate the poster for two illustrations. The students may work alone or in pairs, with one child illustrating the proud attitude and another the humble. When the children are finished, let them explain their illustrations to the rest of the class and then display the posters in the room.

# 22 ( Aspects Of Prayer )

OBJECTIVE: To help children learn about the various elements of prayer

*Appropriate for ages 9 to 12 (and the entire congregation)*

Lead your students into real communion with God by helping them learn to express their needs and thoughts to Him. Teach them that because God is interested in everything about our lives — whether we are concerned about a situation or we are joyful or we simply want to praise Him — we can pray in ways that show these different aspects.

Real communication with God will take place as the children understand the many facets of prayer. These can be best understood with the help of the following acronym:

**A**doration
**C**onfession
**T**hanksgiving
**S**upplication

Plan a five-week study of this concept with your students. Write out the words on the chalkboard each class session, but focus on one term each week. Begin by explaining the word to your students:

Our word "adore" actually comes from the Latin verb that means "to pray." Adoration is worshipping God with awe and admiration. It is showing our love to Him.

The term " 'fess up" is one which your students may have heard or even used. When we confess something to God, we are admitting our wrong-doing or a poor attitude. We not only confess our sin when we ask Jesus to be our Saviour, but we also need to come before God and ask His forgiveness when we make wrong choices.

Giving thanks is perhaps the easiest element of prayer for children, especially younger ones, to understand. What boys and girls should realize, however, is that we need to give thanks for everything. Even when we have unhappy feelings we should thank God for His understanding of our feelings. This serves to focus our attention away from ourselves and onto His love for us.

Supplication is a big word, as is petition, but they both mean the same thing: to make a request

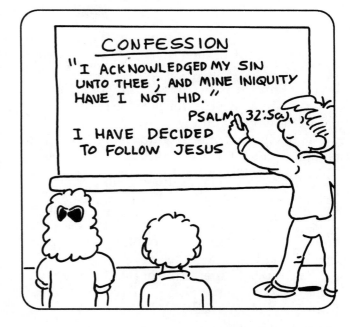

before God. Children can ask God for many things, such as help with a problem at school, or for peace in the midst of family troubles. Emphasize to your students that God keeps our best interests at heart when He answers our prayers.

After explaining the aspect of prayer on which you are focusing for the day, divide the class into groups. Using the Bible and perhaps your church's hymnbook, ask the students to find as many verses or phrases as they can which illustrate the element of prayer. The children may write these expressions on the board.

To make the lesson more personal for the children, ask each student to name one thing for which he can pray that relates to the featured word of the acronym. For instance, one may want to pray with adoration unto God. Another may choose to confess that he cheated on a test at school. Allow some time for talking with God at the close of the session, focusing on the element of prayer taught that day.

# 23 Family Prayer Book

OBJECTIVE: To learn to pray for various needs and to encourage family prayer time

*Appropriate for ages 8 to 12*

Juniors will enjoy making — and benefit from — a prayer book of their own that can be shared with the entire family. The book will help them become familiar with ways to pray for a number of occasions as well as develop the regular practice of praying for others.

You will need at least a dozen pieces of plain or lined paper for each student in your class. These sheets will serve as the main contents of the books, on which the children will write prayers for various occasions. On the day you are ready to make the books, make sure you have gathered enough resources for the students to find prayers they would like to include.

Pass out the paper to the pupils, then provide some books on prayer that you have checked out from your church library. (If such a resource center is not available, check to see if the public library has anything you might be able to use.) Allow the children time to look through the books to find prayers they might want to include in their own prayer book.

As the students make their selections, suggest that they try to think of different "chapters" to put the prayers in. For example, the books could include table graces, bedtime prayers, morning prayers, and prayers for special days like Thanksgiving, Christmas and Easter. Provide strips of construction paper about 1 by 1 1/2 inches and instruct the children to write the chapter headings near the top half. On the first page of each chapter, the pupils will glue the title at the right edge, in succession so that the titles can be read easily (refer to the illustration).

To supplement the prayers found in the books, the children may use any that they write on their own, those composed by other class members, or some which the class work out together.

Suggest that the students include a section for listing prayer requests with places to check off the answers to these requests. The boys and girls should also make a list of family members and include any special needs for which they can pray. In this way the children can take the books home and use them with family devotion time. As other family members see how important prayer is to your students, they will want to make it important in their own lives.

Give each student two pieces of construction paper to be the front and back of his book. Either staple all the pages together or punch holes along the left edge and tie a piece of yarn through each hole. Direct the children to write the title "My Family Prayer Book" on the front. They may decorate the cover with stickers or their own original drawings.

# 24 **Prayer Power Game**

OBJECTIVE: To help children recognize the helps and hindrances to a consistent prayer life

*Appropriate for age 9 to teens*

While we realize the need to communicate with God on a consistent basis, many times we face certain obstacles that make it difficult to pray regularly. This is true for children as well as adults. Playing with friends, watching television, even doing homework can take up so much of the child's time that he forgets to set aside time for prayer, or he may be hindered by the idea that we only pray during church.

The "Prayer Power" Game will help the children in your class recognize, and thus hopefully avoid, various actions and attitudes that would keep them from prayer. Scattered among these are situations which could help foster a better prayer life. The "Blast Off!" cards ask various questions from Scripture about prayer.

To set up the game for your class, duplicate the game board and tape or glue it to the inside of a manila file folder. You may color and laminate the board, if you wish. Tape a 2 by 3 inch rectangle of construction paper to the board to create a pocket for the "Blast Off!" cards. Cut out the cards from pages 35-36 (laminate first if you wish), then

put the cards inside the pocket. Follow the instructions given on page 34 for the markers and spinner. Directions for the game itself are on the board.

# PRAYER POWER

## Directions:

Power up your prayer life by propelling your spacecraft from the Starship to Planet Prayer! Take turns using the spinner to move forward. You have the opportunity to use warp speed if you land on a Blast Off space. Take a card and, using fuel from the Bible, answer the question. If you are right, you may move forward to the next available blank space. An incorrect answer will put you back to where you were before. Watch out for hindrances to prayer along the flight path, because they will delay your journey! The first player to reach Planet Prayer wins the game.

PLANET
PRAYER

Unforgiving attitude
Miss a turn

BLAST OFF!

Pray for your homeroom teacher
Go ahead 1

BLAST OFF!

Just don't feel like praying
Go back 2

BLAST OFF!

BLAST OFF!

Struggling with disbelief
Go back 4

BLAST OFF!

BLAST OFF!

Embarrassed to pray in public
Go back 2

BLAST OFF!

BLAST OFF!

God answered your prayer request
Go ahead 4

BLAST OFF!

32

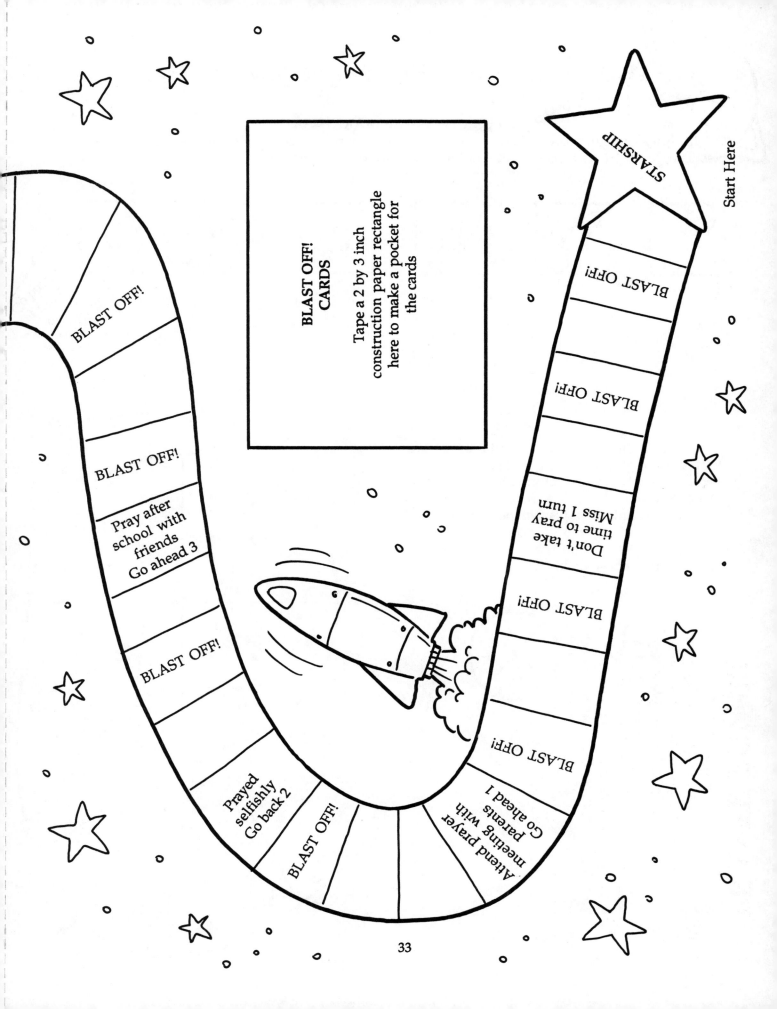

Start Here

STARSHIP

BLAST OFF!

BLAST OFF!

Don't take
time to pray
Miss 1 turn

BLAST OFF!

BLAST OFF!

Attend prayer
meeting with
parents
Go ahead 1

BLAST OFF!

Prayed
selfishly
Go back 2

BLAST OFF!

Pray after
school with
friends
Go ahead 3

BLAST OFF!

BLAST OFF!

BLAST OFF!
CARDS

Tape a 2 by 3 inch
construction paper rectangle
here to make a pocket for
the cards

33

# Markers and Spinner for Prayer Power Game

## PRAYER POWER MARKERS

Duplicate and glue to poster board or cardboard, then laminate or cover with clear adhesive-backed plastic, if desired. Cut apart one marker for each child to use in the game.

## PRAYER POWER SPINNER

Duplicate and glue to poster board or cardboard, then laminate or cover with clear adhesive-backed plastic, if desired. Attach a paper clip to the spinner circle by running a paper fastener through the paper clip. (See diagram.) Tape down the prongs of the paper fastener on the underside of the spinner to prevent scratching.

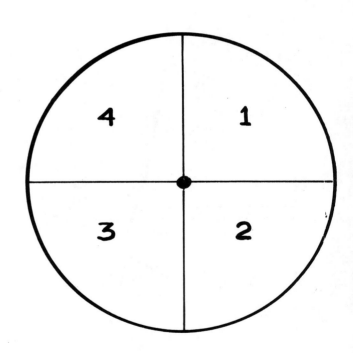

| | | |
|---|---|---|
| My house shall be called a house of _____ for all people.<br>Isaiah 56:7 | What promise is found in Psalm 91:15? | What will happen when we search with all our heart?<br>Jeremiah 29:13 |
| The Spirit makes intercession according to what?<br>Romans 8:27 | What are we to pray without?<br>I Thessalonians 5:17 | What is necessary for one to be healed?<br>James 5:16 |
| According to Matthew 7:7, what will happen when we pray? | Why did Elijah want God to hear his prayer?<br>I Kings 18:37 | We will receive from God what we ask because _____.<br>I John 3:22 |
| What are we to do to keep from entering into temptation?<br>Matthew 26:41 | What promise is found in Isaiah 58:9? | What are we not to use when we pray?<br>Matthew 6:7 |
| Luke 18:1 says men ought always to do what? | Isaiah 65:24 says God will do what when we pray? | What did Daniel do when he went into his house?<br>Daniel 6:10 |
| What will be full when we ask in Jesus' name?<br>John 16:24 | What does God say He will do for His people if they pray?<br>II Chronicles 7:14 | What will God show us when we pray?<br>Jeremiah 33:3 |

| | | |
|---|---|---|
| Ye shall seek Me, and find Me | He shall call upon Me, and I will answer him: I will be with him in trouble; I will deliver him, and honour him. | Prayer |
| Confess your faults one to another, and pray one for another | Ceasing | The will of God |
| We keep His commandments, and do those things that are pleasing in His sight | That this people may know that Thou art the Lord God, and that Thou hast turned their heart back again. | Ask, and it shall be given you; seek, and ye shall find; knock, and it shall be opened unto you. |
| Vain repetitions | Then shalt thou call, and the LORD shall answer; thou shalt cry, and He shall say, Here I am. | Watch and pray |
| He kneeled upon his knees three times a day, and prayed, and gave thanks before his God | And it shall come to pass, that before they call, I will answer; and while they are yet speaking, I will hear. | To pray, and not to faint |
| Great and mighty things | Forgive their sin and heal their land | Our joy |

# 25 ( Prayer Pockets )

OBJECTIVE: To create a willingness to pray for others

*Appropriate for ages 6 to 9*

Create a colorful bulletin board that will make your students want to pray for the requests made in your class.

Use brightly colored paper to cover the board and write out the heading "Prayer Pockets" using a heavy felt-tip marker or pre-cut letters. Cut regular mailing envelopes in half and print your students' names on the "pockets." Make a few extra for visitors and one for blank cards. Staple or tape the pockets to the board.

In class, give out several 3 by 5 inch cards to each boy and girl and ask the students to write out their prayer requests. Collect the cards and divide them between the pockets, one to three cards in each. The blank cards should always be available for the children to write out new prayer requests.

When you are ready for prayer time, tell the children to remove the cards from their pockets and come back to sit in a circle. Go around the circle and allow each child to pray for the requests on his cards. If any children show a hesitancy to pray out loud, let them know that they can still pray for the requests silently.

Rotate the cards each week. Be sure to let the children offer prayers of thanksgiving when their requests are answered.

# 26 Match-A-Prayer

**OBJECTIVE:** To help children realize they can pray in any situation in life

*Appropriate for ages 9 to 12*

Write the following verse on the chalkboard or wherever the members of your class can see it best: "Pray in the Spirit on all occasions with all kinds of prayers and requests." Ephesians 6:18a (NIV)

Discuss with your class what kinds of situations we can pray about. You might hear answers that relate to family, school, or sickness. Explain to the children that God wants us to pray about anything, no matter how big or small. He has the power to work in whatever way He chooses.

Say the verse together with your class, then use the matching game below to reinforce the lesson. Place a half sheet of paper over the top of this page before duplicating to cover answers and so that only the game will show. The answers are: Jonah - 5; Hezekiah - 7; Elijah - 6; Nehemiah - 8; Abraham - 1; Moses - 3; Jacob - 2; Solomon - 4. The leftover answers are David and Jeremiah.

# Match-A-Prayer Game

The following are examples of prayers mentioned in the Old Testament. They show several different situations when people addressed God in prayer. Use your Bibles to look up the answers. Match the numbers of the prayer prayed with the name of the person who prayed. There will be two names left over which you do not use:

## Names

_____ Jonah
_____ Hezekiah
_____ Elijah
_____ Nehemiah
_____ David
_____ Abraham
_____ Moses
_____ Jeremiah
_____ Jacob
_____ Solomon

## Prayed For . . .

1. God's wrath to be averted from the cities of the plain (Genesis 18:23-33).
2. protection against Esau (Genesis 32:9-12).
3. Miriam when she was stricken with leprosy (Numbers 12:10-13).
4. dedication of the temple (I Kings 8:22, 59).
5. deliverance from the whale (Jonah 2:1-9).
6. God to overcome Baal (I Kings 18:36-37).
7. protection against Sennacherib (II Kings 19:15-20).
8. the great affliction of his people (Nehemiah 1:3-11).

# 27 (God Wants To Listen)

OBJECTIVE: To role-play a situation that illustrates the importance of communication

*Appropriate for ages 4 to 9*

Help young children learn that God wants us to talk to Him anytime and from anywhere — at home, at church, in the car, out-of-doors — it doesn't matter when or where. And just as the people around us listen and answer when we talk to them, God always hears His children when they pray.

Explain to the students that although we cannot actually see God, He is with us everywhere we go and He wants us to talk to Him. We would feel left out or ignored if we were with someone and he or she acted like we weren't there.

Role-play a situation like this with your class: have each student take turns trying to communicate with his classmates, but tell the rest of the children not to look at or talk with him. After several boys and girls have had a turn, ask them how they feel. They will probably say they feel frustrated and ignored, and maybe even a little angry.

Share with the children that God also feels forgotten and neglected when we don't talk to Him or acknowledge His presence. He may not necessarily be angry with us, but He does miss our fellowship when we are not taking notice of

Him. Emphasize that God never leaves us alone. He is always ready to hear our problems, our needs, our praise, and our thanksgiving. He wants to share in everything we do and to help us in every way He can. All we have to do is talk with Him through prayer.

39

# 28 Prayer Reminder Pyramids

OBJECTIVE: To create a visual reminder to pray for others

*Appropriate for ages 6 to 9*

Let your class make prayer reminder pyramids to take home. The students may use them in daily devotion time to remember to pray for friends and loved ones.

The pyramid patterns below have three sides on which the children may write the names of people or situations they want to pray about. Duplicate the pyramid pattern so that each child has one, and remember to include one for yourself. Let the students glue the pattern onto construction paper and cut along the solid lines. Give each child a pencil to write down his prayer requests, then show the class a pyramid you have finished so that the students can see how to fold along the dotted lines. Provide paste or glue for the pupils to put together the appropriate sections as directed.

Tell your students to place the pyramid on a dresser, desk, or night stand in their rooms and to turn the pyramid each day to put a different name

at the front side for special prayer.

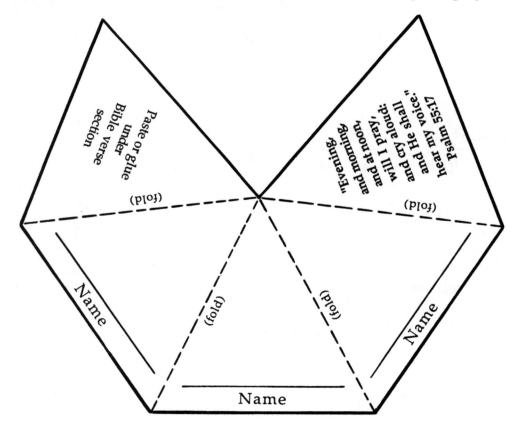

Paste or glue under Bible verse section

(fold)

"Evening, and morning, and at noon, will I pray, and cry aloud: and He shall hear my voice." Psalm 55:17

(fold)

Name

(fold)

(fold)

Name

Name

# 29 Moments Of Meditation

**OBJECTIVE:** To discuss with your class what Jesus meant when He prayed the Lord's Prayer

*Appropriate for age 9 to teens (and the entire congregation)*

Older children and teens can be drawn into a meaningful time of worship and discussion with this idea. As students gather for class have a recording of hymns softly playing in the background. When all the pupils have arrived, put on a recording of "The Lord's Prayer" and ask each one to close his eyes and think about the words so they can be discussed later. When the last note sounds, don't be surprised to find the room filled with quiet students who are ready to learn.

The Lord's Prayer (Matthew 6:9-15) is often sung or recited but not always explained. Discuss with your class what it means. See if your students notice the Lord's excellent teaching method of showing the disciples how to pray instead of just telling them.

Next discuss the prayer itself starting with "Our Father Which art in heaven." Emphasize to the class that Jesus identifies Himself with us when He says *our* Father.

Then comes "Hallowed be Thy Name." Ask your students if they think God's name is treated with the respect It deserves. If they answer in the negative, have them suggest ways that they can help change that, whether at home, in school, with the ball team, or wherever.

Tell your students to think about the next phrase of the Lord's Prayer. Ask, "Do we really want God's kingdom to come and His will to be done in our lives?" Challenge your students to think about this question seriously. Ask for comments as to how God's will can be done in each student's life.

Each day we need to follow the Lord's Prayer by thanking God for His daily provision. Of course God does not personally cook our meals for us, but He does provide the natural resources for our "daily bread." Ask your students, "Can you think of anything that we eat that God has not provided the ingredients to prepare?"

The next phrase of the prayer directs our

attention toward forgiveness. Ask the children, "Is it more difficult to apologize yourself or to forgive someone when he has not shown that he is sorry?" Explain to the class that this is just one area where Christians need to ask for God's help to change our attitudes from what our normal human reactions would be.

"Lead us not into temptation." The temptation to go our own way is a part of us from the time we are born. When we ask the Lord to become our Savior, this does not mean that Satan gives up on us. Have your students share why we need to constantly seek God's help to ward off temptation to do wrong.

Lastly, share the joy with your class that God is Ever-Powerful and that He will reign forever. And as Jesus included praise in His prayer, so should we.

End the discussion by listening to the Lord's Prayer again. This time the students should hear it with a deeper level of understanding and meditation.

# 30 Bible Prayer Search-And-Draw

OBJECTIVE: To help students visually identify the various situations when biblical people prayed

*Appropriate for age 9 to teens*

Who prayed for what in the Bible? Use this picture charade game to see if your older students can quickly identify the person and the place or time associated with several biblical prayers.

You will need some kind of timer, such as a watch with a second hand, and something for the students to draw on. A dry erase board with markers would work best, but if this is not available, a large pad of paper with pens or a chalkboard and chalk may be used.

Write the following Scripture references on slips of paper, then fold the slips of paper and place them in an envelope or paper bag. (You might want to include the short description of the passage with the reference.)

When all the materials are ready, divide your class into two groups. Choose a team to begin the game and select someone to go first. Placing his hand into the envelope or bag without seeing what is written on the slips of paper, the student will pick out a reference. He will have two minutes to look up the verse(s) and decide how he can draw the prayer scene for his team members to guess what it is. When he is ready, set the timer and let him begin drawing. Just as in regular charades, the student will not be allowed to speak, but if his team members say any part of the answer, such as the biblical person's name or where the prayer took place, the student may write the word down.

The team will have five minutes to guess the right answer for 100 points. If, however, the correct answer is not given within that time, the other team will score 50 points provided the team members can guess the right answer without any further drawing. If neither team guesses correctly, the score remains as it was and the second team picks a reference and chooses a member to draw.

Continue to let the groups take turns back and forth. The team with the most points at the end of the game wins. You may want to clarify to your students, "Competition is not as important as

understanding what you are drawing." Discuss a few of the prayers with them, emphasizing the idea that we can pray in any situation with confidence that God will listen.

**Bible Prayer Search-And-Draw References:**
- Luke 23:33-34 (Jesus on the cross)
- Acts 9:1-9 (Saul on the Damascus Road)
- Jonah 1:11-2:1 (Jonah thrown overboard and swallowed by the whale)
- Acts 7:54-60 (Stephen while he was being stoned)
- Exodus 32:30-35 (Moses after Aaron made the golden calf)
- I Samuel 1:9-17 (Hannah praying in the tabernacle)
- Acts 16:25-31 (Paul and Silas in jail)
- Daniel 6:7-13 (Daniel defying the king's orders)
- Luke 22:39-46 (Jesus in the garden before His death)
- I Kings 18:30-38 (Elijah before the prophets of Baal)

# 31 Benedictions

*Appropriate for ages 9 to 12*

Juniors will enjoy learning these benedictions which can be used at different times to open their classes or conclude them. The students might even want to adopt one in particular to use for an entire quarter or month.

**Crusader's Benediction**: "Let the words of my mouth, and the meditation of my heart, be acceptable in thy sight, O Lord, my strength, and my Redeemer." (Psalm 19:14)

**Ambassador's Benediction**: "The Lord bless thee, and keep thee: the Lord make His face shine upon thee, and be gracious unto thee: the Lord lift up His countenance upon thee, and give thee peace." (Numbers 6:24-26)

**Mizpah Benediction**: "The Lord watch between me and thee, when we are absent one from another." (Genesis 31:49)

**Apostolic Benediction**: "The grace of the Lord Jesus Christ, and the love of God, and the communion of the Holy Ghost, be with you all. Amen." (II Corinthians 13:14)

**Shepherd's Benediction**: "Now the God of peace, that brought again from the dead our Lord Jesus, that great Shepherd of the sheep, through the blood of the everlasting covenant, make you perfect in every good work to do His will, working in you that which is wellpleasing in His sight,

THE LORD BLESS THEE, AND KEEP THEE...

through Jesus Christ; to Whom be glory for ever and ever. Amen." (Hebrews 13:20, 21)

**Pastoral Benediction**: "Now unto him that is able to keep you from falling, and to present you faultless before the presence of His glory with exceeding joy, to the only wise God our Savior, be glory and majesty, dominion and power, both now and ever. Amen." (Jude 24, 25)

# 32 Paper Plate Prayer Reminders

OBJECTIVE: To help young children view God as a Friend to Whom they can always turn

*Appropriate for ages 4 to 8*

The character of God is one that takes on a variety of roles — He is our Creator, our Prince of Peace, our Defender, and so on. The role which children can relate to most, however, is probably Friend. A friend interacts with us day-by-day, always ready to listen, to lend a helping hand, to comfort, and to share. To help young children understand that the Lord offers Friendship and that they can talk with Him at any time and from any place, discuss these ideas with them. Then help them create Paper Plate Prayer Reminders to remember God's Friendship.

Before class time duplicate the pattern for clock hands and the poem "My Special Friend" for each student. Help the children cut these out. Give each student a paper plate (this kind works better than styrofoam) or a circle of construction paper and show an example of how to write in the numbers one through twelve. (You may need to do this for younger children.) Provide glue or a glue stick so the children can position the poem at the top of the plate just underneath the numbers. Poke a paper fastener first through the holes in the clock hands and then through the center of the plate. Separate and bend the two parts of the fastener, then put tape over both to prevent

scratching.

Read the poem with the children and ask them to put the prayer reminders in their rooms, on the refrigerator, or anywhere that can help them remember to pray. Then sing "What A Friend We Have In Jesus" together.

**My Special Friend**

Anytime, anywhere, I can talk to God.
When I'm glad, when I'm sad,
I can talk to God.
Sometimes on my knees I pray,
Sometimes as I work or play.
When I need Him through the day,
My best Friend is He.

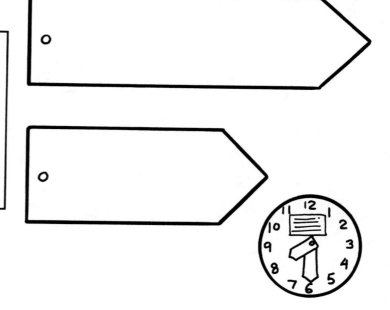

# 33 Seven Days Without Prayer Poster

**OBJECTIVE:** To visually demonstrate the need for regular prayer

*Appropriate for age 9 to teens (and the entire congregation)*

As the saying goes, a picture is worth a thousand words, so use a "picture" to illustrate the need for daily prayer in the lives of believers.

You will need a sheet of poster board and some pieces of chenille wire. Draw a one-month calendar onto the poster board, making sure to leave plenty of space at the bottom for the slogan. Using a heavy felt-tip marker, pre-cut letters or letters you make out of construction paper, spell out the words "SEVEN DAYS WITHOUT PRAYER . . . MAKE ONE WEAK!

Bend the wire to form seven stick figures that gradually show a progression from running to lying down. Staple the figures to the poster, positioning the first over the four Sundays, the next on Monday, etc. Display this "miniature sermon" where everyone in your class can see it.

---

# 34 Prayer Alphabet

**OBJECTIVE:** To create a poster using the ABCs to list things we should pray for

*Appropriate for ages 6 to 9*

Young children usually have at least one alphabet book in their collection covering the ABCs of nature or animals or occupations, etc. Let your students create their own alphabet to guide the class during prayer time.

Use a large sheet of poster board or a long sheet of butcher paper tacked to a wall. At the top of the sheet print "OUR PRAYER ALPHABET — THIS IS WHAT WE PRAY FOR." Then use a heavy felt-tip marker or pre-cut letters to print the alphabet, either across the top or down in columns, allowing space to write a word by each letter.

In class, allow the children to contribute the names of things to pray for. These can be as general or as specific as necessary so that the alphabet is complete. If you wish, let the children illustrate the poster with pictures that they draw themselves or cut from magazines.

45

# 35 The Lord's Prayer In Color

OBJECTIVE: To show the meaning of the Lord's Prayer in a colorful presentation using candles

*Appropriate for age 6 to teens (and the entire congregation)*

The Bible says that God's Word is a light unto our feet. We want to turn on that light for our children by helping them to understand the Lord's Prayer. Uncovering the meaning of the Lord's Prayer through a candlelight service can be a beautiful and effective way to accomplish this.

Read through the following discourse several times so that you are familiar with it. You will notice that each phrase of the Lord's Prayer is represented with a different colored candle. As you explain each phrase to your class, you will bring out a candle of that particular color so that by the end of the lesson, the children may be able to look at the row of colors, name what they symbolize, and possibly recite the Lord's Prayer. More importantly though, your students will have a better grasp of what God's Son meant as He showed by example how we should pray.

To make the presentation before your class, set up a candelabra (your church may have one that is kept for weddings) to hold each candle after you light it. Or, if you want to allow your students more participation, let volunteers come up to hold the candles. To help keep the wax from getting on their fingers, cut out construction paper "doughnuts" ahead of time and slide them up to the middle of the candles.

As you make the presentation, you may want to use a record or tape player to have the music of the Lord's Prayer playing in the background. For a stronger effect, turn off the lights and use a small flashlight or piano light for reading.

1. **"Our Father"** (white candle; this should be the longest one used to show that God is supreme over all) — This first one will represent God, Who is light. How dark the world would be if this light should flicker or go out, but God has promised that He will never leave us alone.

2. **"Which Art in Heaven"** (blue) — The color blue reminds us of the blue heavens above us. God watches over us from Heaven, but at the same time He is always with us wherever we go.

3. **"Hallowed Be Thy Name"** (green) — Green is the most enduring of colors. The cedar and pine trees are green all year long. Green is the everlast-

ing color. The Name of God is everlasting, and it will endure forever. His Name will be spoken and loved forever. He is holy, and we must keep His Name holy.

4. **"Thy Kingdom Come"** (purple) — Purple is the royal color. The decorations of a throne are in this majestic color and so are the robes of a king. Our God is the King of Kings, and just as a king reigns over his subjects, God rules over the whole world. He wants to be Lord of our lives. We must give ourselves to God so that His kingdom can live in our hearts.

5. **"Thy Will Be Done In Earth, As It Is In Heaven"** (brown) — The color of the earth is brown. God made the earth and all its many people, so He knows what is best for this world. We need to let go of our selfishness and let God do His will in everything.

6. **"Give Us This Day Our Daily Bread"** (yellow) — When God created the world, He also provided food for us. This is a prayer for our physical needs and the yellow candle represents the grain which makes our bread. We need to bring our specific needs before Him and believe His promises that He will hear and answer.

7. **"Forgive Us Our Debts As We Forgive Our Debtors"** (silver) — The color silver represents

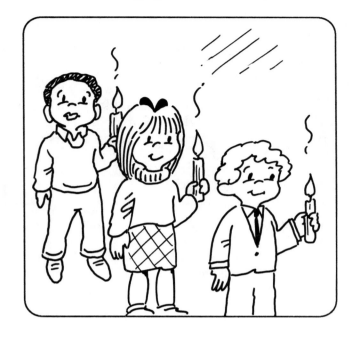

46

the coins we use to pay our debts. This phrase, however, also refers to spiritual debts and debts against our fellow man. We need to grant forgiveness to others so that we can receive the forgiveness God has for us.

8. **"Lead Us Not Into Temptation"** (black) — If we yield to temptation, it will lead us into the blackness of sin. The Bible tells us the wages of sin is death. We need to pray every day that God will put His armor of protection around us to fight against temptation.

9. **"But Deliver Us From Evil"** (red) — If we do yield to temptation, God offers deliverance from sin through His Son. Jesus shed His blood when He died for us on the cross. Red reminds us of the sacrifice He made so that we could live, if we just believe in Him and accept Him as our Savior.

10. **"For Thine Is The Kingdom, And The Power"** (gold) — God's heavenly kingdom will not need the light of the sun or moon, because the Bible says the glory of God gives it light. God has never-ending power to do all the things we ask of Him in prayer, if we trust and obey.

11. **"And The Glory For ever"** (orange) — Orange is the dominant color in a glorious sunset, which reminds us of the glory of God. The great painters of the Middle Ages colored the flame in the "burning bush" orange, which in their day was understood to stand for Jehovah. That flame also brings light, which reminds us of our first candle.

Now we have all the symbols of the Lord's Prayer shining before us. No prayer is so full of divine radiance as the Lord's Prayer. Every time we pray it, may we think of all these wonderful truths about our Heavenly Father.

Close by repeating the Lord's Prayer together.

# 36 ( Who Prayed What? )

*Appropriate for ages 9 to 12*

We can pray many kinds of prayers. There are prayers of confession when we acknowledge sin that has entered our lives. There are intercessory prayers which are prayers on the behalf of others. Our prayers may be for praise and thanksgiving or for a specific need. Sometimes we may be asked to lead the group in public prayer, and at other times we may pray privately, alone with God.

Let the children use their Bibles to find out who prayed the different kinds of prayers listed below. Give the Scripture reference first, then ask the question. This can be done as a game by having the first person to get the right answer raise his hand. Give points for the first correct answer.

a.  I built an altar on Mt. Carmel. The prophets of Baal also built an altar there. I prayed and God consumed my sacrifice with fire. Who am I? (Elijah — I Kings 18:19, 30-40)

b.  I prayed for a child. I promised that I would give this child back to the Lord. The child, Samuel, served with Eli in the temple. Who am I? (Hannah — I Samuel 1:10-11, 20-28)

c.  I prayed for the early churches to whom I wrote. I often prayed in prison or while suffering hardships. One of my well-known prayers was for the church at Ephesus. Who am I? (Paul — Ephesians 3:1-21)

d.  I prayed for God to save a city if righteous men could be found there. The name of the city was Sodom. My nephew, Lot, lived there. Who am I? (Abraham — Genesis 18:23-33)

e.  I prayed for the captive Jews. My Babylonian name was Belteshazzar. I was thrown into the den of lions because I would not stop praying. Who am I? (Daniel — Daniel 1:7; 6:11-13, 16; 9:4)

f.  I prayed for God to keep me from dying. The prophet Isaiah brought me a message from the Lord. The Lord let me live fifteen years longer. Who am I? (Hezekiah — Isaiah 38:1-5)

g.  My husband was a priest named Zacharias. God answered our prayer for a child. Our son John was born about six months before Jesus. Who am I? (Elisabeth — Luke 1:5-25)

h.  The Lord told me to preach at Nineveh. Instead I headed for Tarshish and was thrown overboard from the boat. I prayed to God while inside the stomach of a fish. Who am I? (Jonah — Jonah 1:3, 2:1-9)

# 37 [ Greeting Card Prayer List ]

OBJECTIVE: To make a visual reminder to pray for friends and family

*Appropriate for age 9 to teens*

Children receive greeting cards throughout the year for their birthdays, holidays, and sometimes when they are ill. Many cards also come from schoolmates and teachers on St. Valentine's Day. Unless the child is prone to keep things that may be of "sentimental value," the cards are probably thrown away after sitting for a week on the dresser. Put the cards to a better use by turning them into prayer reminders.

Suggest to your students that they start a collection of the cards they receive and help them decorate a shoe box or file box so that they may keep the cards handy. Instruct the boys and girls to take out the first card each day and to pray for the friend or relative who sent it. If the card is from a schoolmate, the child may be familiar with any current situations which the friend needs prayer for. If the card is from a relative, the child may ask his parents about any special needs that relatives may have. After prayer time, the card should be placed at the back so that a fresh card comes up for the next day.

The prayer "list" will grow as the children

continue to receive more cards, and this project will creatively help your students develop a daily practice of praying for others, beginning with the people with whom they come into contact most.

# 38 Prayer Partners

OBJECTIVE: To encourage your students to pray for each other

*Appropriate for ages 6 to 12 (and the entire congregation)*

One of the most wonderful aspects of prayer is that we can bring before God the concerns of others around us, and He will listen. When we intercede for our friends and family, even for those whom we do not know personally, we experience a certain kinship toward the other person that says, "I care about you."

To encourage your students to pray on this level, develop prayer partnerships among them.

Write the verse "Where two or three are gathered together in My Name, there am I in the midst of them" (Matthew 18:20) on a chalkboard or poster board so the pupils can see it. Read the verse out loud with the students and ask what it means to them.

Next, divide your class into two groups. Have each child in Group One write his or her name on a slip of paper. Put these slips into a paper bag. Instruct the children in Group Two to take turns reaching into the bag to select a name. The students are now paired into groups of prayer partners.

Let the children get together for ten minutes or so to share some things about themselves. Since many of their initial requests will probably be for their families, the students should write down the names of their family members for each other. They may also share any requests or praises they have at the moment and then take turns praying for each other's needs.

Allow a few minutes at the beginning of each class session for the prayer partners to meet together. Encourage the children to keep their partnership active during the week; for instance,

they could get together after school for prayer. You might want to send a note home to their parents asking permission for them to share phone numbers. This way they can call at times when it may otherwise be difficult to meet in person and still have a chance to share their needs and praises.

The students may reinforce their partnerships in another way by keeping small notebooks. This will help them remember the requests throughout the week as they refer to the notebook when they pray alone. If they wish, they can write the Bible verse on the front to remind them that God always hears them when they pray.

# 39  Paraphrase A Bible Prayer

OBJECTIVE: To help children understand the meanings of biblical prayers

*Appropriate for age 9 to teens*

The popularity of cartoon and television characters today may be attributed to the fact that children can see and hear them every day. People from the Bible, however, are not as easily visualized. This may hinder children from recognizing the men, women, boys and girls who lived thousands of years ago as people who were like us today.

To help your students relate to these biblical people, direct the children to read selected prayers from the Bible and to rewrite the prayers in their own words. Ask the boys and girls to share how they see what role prayer took in the life of the biblical character. This will also help them to understand the message of the prayer itself.

Some Bible prayers to consider are:
- I Kings 17:17-24 — Elijah prays for the widow's son to live again;
- I Chronicles 29:10-20 — David praises the Lord that his people gave willingly for the building of the temple;
- Psalm 51 — David confesses sin in his life and asks the Lord for forgiveness;
- I Kings 3:6-9 — Solomon asks the Lord for wisdom;

- Luke 1:46-55 — Mary rejoices that she is chosen to be Jesus' mother;
- John 17 — Jesus prays before His death;
- Colossians 1:9-14 — Paul prays for the Colossians to mature as Christians.

# 40 ( Table Blessing )

OBJECTIVE: To create a visual reminder for young children to thank God at mealtime

*Appropriate for ages 3 to 6*

Use the pattern on page 53 to make one cup and saucer for each student, or duplicate the pattern and let the children themselves cut out the pieces. Cut along the dotted line on the cup to make two flaps. Insert the flaps through the slit in the saucer and fold in opposite directions under the saucer. Tape the flaps to help the cup stand upright.

Ask the children if they have ever received a gift from someone. Did they say "thank you" for the gift? Explain that God created everything necessary to provide food for us — the ground, the rain, the seeds that grow into plants and grains, the animals, etc. — and that we should thank Him for looking after us in this way. We also want to ask Him to help our bodies use the food to make us strong and healthy.

If you have the time and resources available, set up a "tea party" for the students with real cups and saucers. Pour out juice or milk (preferably instead of Kool-Aid, a product of human creativity rather than God's) for each child, and offer a snack of sliced fruits or vegetables. Before the children are ready to eat, say the table blessing together. Some families join hands when they pray, so you may want to incorporate this idea as well.

Encourage the children to set the cup and saucer blessing reminder on their own dining room table at home. For those who come from families which are not already in the practice of giving thanks to God at mealtime, this reminder may serve to get them started.

52

### TABLE BLESSING

Dear Lord,
We thank You, Father, for this food
And pray You'll bless it to our good;
Help us live Your Name to praise
In all we do through all our days.
Amen.

(fold forward)  (cut)  (fold back)

Fold flaps in opposite directions underneath
saucer and tape them down

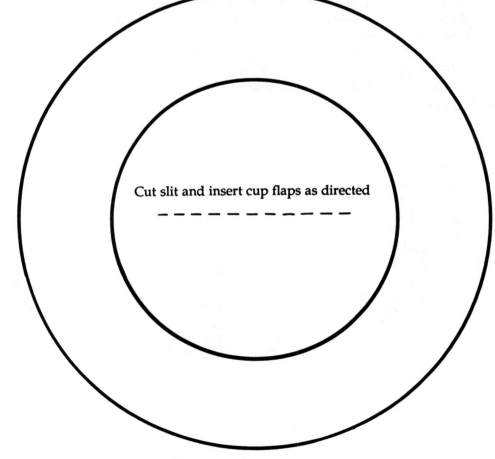

Cut slit and insert cup flaps as directed

53

# 41 Prayer For The Church

OBJECTIVE: To make your students aware of the needs in your church

*Appropriate for ages 9 to 12*

The children whom we teach in Sunday School, mid-week activities, and Bible clubs are just as much a part of the church as the adults who sing in the choir, take the offering, and call on visitors. To help our boys and girls see church as more than just a social gathering, we need to let them take an active role in the life of the church.

As a step in this direction, ask your students to write prayers that relate to your church and its needs. Every church has needs, simply because the people who are a part of it have needs. The needs can be physical, material, financial, and of course spiritual. If your students are aware that Mrs. Smith is in the hospital for surgery or that $3,000 needs to come in the offering by the end of the month, they are certainly capable of going to God in prayer about these things.

You may want to ask the pastor to share with your class any needs he is aware of. You may also choose to take your class on a walking tour of the church to see if there are material needs represented in the building and furnishings.

To show the congregation that they are interested in praying for the church's needs, the children could recite their prayers during worship services or have their written prayers reproduced in the bulletin or placed on an attractive bulletin board in the church. This activity will not only teach your students about prayer, but it will also help them feel a part of their church. The exercise will open a way for the children to help meet the various needs through their awareness of them and prayers for them.

# 42 How Does God Answer?

**OBJECTIVE:** To show that God answers prayer in a variety of ways

*Appropriate for ages 7 to 10*

Ask your students, "When you pray do you expect to hear from God? Do you know that we must listen for God's answer when we talk to Him?"

To help illustrate this concept, use two play telephones (make sure they have "ringers"). Choose two student volunteers to come forward and hold the two phones, one across the room from the other. The first pupil will "dial" the number to the other phone and begin talking. Tell the second child to listen quietly, not making a sound. After a minute or so of talking, the first student will hang up and sit back down.

When the second pupil returns to his seat, ask the class to describe what happened. The boys and girls will probably be quick to point out that the second child never got a chance to respond to what the first student was saying.

Discuss with your class the idea that prayer is two-way communication. We are free to talk with God whenever we wish, but we also need to listen to what He says in response! When we pray, in any situation, we should be prepared to hear God's answer and to accept it.

Your class may wonder at this point, "How does God answer our requests?" Explain that sometimes He says "Yes," sometimes "No," and sometimes "Wait a while." Biblical examples may help your students understand this better, so use the following illustrations:

Elijah asked the Lord to send down fire to consume the sacrifice on the altar. This way, he said, the people could know the Lord is the true God. I Kings 18:37-38 tells us of the Lord's im-

mediate answer. The Lord said, "Yes."

In II Samuel, Chapter 7, David prayed for the privilege of building a house for the Lord, but God said, "No" — that job would be for David's son.

In chapters 7 through 11 in the book of Exodus, Moses went before Pharoah and asked for the children of Israel to be released. Nine times Pharoah hardened his heart toward the Israelites, but the Lord told Moses, "he will let you go from here, and when he does, he will drive you out completely." (Exodus 11:1 NIV) It was a long, difficult "Wait," but in the Lord's time deliverance was indeed complete.

# 43 ( Prayer Mobiles )

OBJECTIVE: To create a visual reminder of things to pray about or thank God for

*Appropriate for ages 6 to 10*

Children love to make mobiles, and these crafts are easy to put together. Let your class make them to help illustrate things we can thank God for or pray about, such as creation, our families, missionaries, teachers, etc.

You will need to ask the children ahead of time to bring a plastic coat hanger from home, and if they wish, pictures of their families and/or friends. For the illustrations, provide magazines and scissors or blank pieces of paper for the children to draw on. Let the children glue their pictures onto colorful pieces of construction paper and use a hole punch at the top. The students can attach the pictures to the hangers by tying various lengths of yarn through the holes in the illustrations and then to the hangers. (Tape yarn strands in place on the hanger to prevent sliding.)

Hang the mobiles in the classroom for a while, then let the children take them home to hang in their rooms.

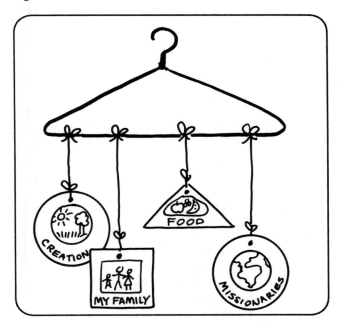

# 44 ( Promise Word Search )

OBJECTIVE: To creatively help children learn God's promise that He will answer our prayers

*Appropriate for ages 7 to 12*

We can trust God to always answer our prayers because He promised in Jeremiah 33:3 that He would. Knowing this promise can help your class develop confidence as the children begin to show more dependence on God.

Help your boys and girls learn the Scripture with the following classroom activity. Reproduce the Promise Word Search on page 57 for each student and instruct the children to find the words of the passage. When they are finished, see how many have memorized the verse. Put a star or sticker on the sheet for any children who can recite the verse.

Answers are on page 64.

# PROMISE WORD SEARCH

God promises to always answer us when we pray. The words of His promise made in Jeremiah 33:3 are hidden in the puzzle below. Can you find them? Draw a loop around each word as you locate it, then try to memorize the verse. It will help you in your prayer life to know that God will always answer when you call on Him.

CALL        UNTO        ME
AND        I        WILL
ANSWER        THEE        AND
SHOW        THEE        GREAT
AND        MIGHTY        THINGS

```
A N D C V F Z R C R D J D E Y G V W V M
D A V A J K C B A N D X L Y W Q A W B I
S B O E B Y Z T H F U F E H S E N C T G
S L T C J D C R A Z G U N T O W D L Q H
D Y M A X A Z H E G C T H E E Z K J P T
M D V N T F O V S W J D P V P Z S K B Y
R L M F F R Z G B W S Q Y M U T Q D L O
Z A B C O U B S W P D N G X C F Q Z O Q
A C C V F M Z U E L T B A K C S H O W A
L S W E B U X Z V A Y K L P J Q X Q A O
P E O T H E E L X J R T L K K R C Y D Z
G W R T B P U L K X D H Q T T M Q D V Z
G Q Y U U G Y A R Q L I E P K Y Q B V X
B P M O F L C C Q Y V N L V D D Z S J K
Y X X E H W Y O V Z H G W X R O H D Z T
J L X F D Z S D T Y W S Y W Z Q U T U Y
P M D L G R E K G L G L S P D L F O J N
B Z R I S X B S D F N X C L L I W V R U
Z D E Y M Y N H M V O B T A E R G H B M
```

# 45 Choral Prayer

OBJECTIVE: To identify with other children by praying together

*Appropriate for ages 9 to 12*

Most of the time we think of prayer as talking with God on a personal basis or in terms of listening to our pastors, teachers, and leaders as they pray out loud for us. However, we can also benefit from praying together as a group. This goes for children as well; because they have so many common experiences — getting along with siblings, trying to obey their parents, making progress at school — they can find reassurance by joining together in prayer.

Divide your class into groups of three or four students. Give each group a sheet of paper and a pencil, then direct the students to formulate a group prayer. Ask them to first think of things they would want to pray about individually and then to put these ideas together into one prayer.

Another way to carry out this lesson would be to assign a Bible passage to each group and direct the boys and girls to develop a prayer based on the passage. Ask them to make the prayer meaningful to them personally. Some passages which would work well for this are Psalm 37:1-9, Romans 12, and I Corinthians 13.

Allow ten minutes or so for the students to work on the assignment, then let each group come forward to read its prayer in unison as a choral group.

# 46 Get In Gear Bulletin Board

OBJECTIVE: To emphasize God's promise to hear our prayers

*Appropriate for ages 7 to 10*

Prepare a bulletin board with the following wording: "When we pray in God's Will, We're really in gear, For we know that God promised He always would hear." (See the illustration.) Duplicate the gear pattern onto colored paper or construction paper for each child in your class and let the students cut out the patterns. Each child should write his name on the top line of the gear and then write below the names of the people or situations he is praying for. Attach the gears to the bulletin board with thumb tacks so they can be turned.

Ask a student to read Proverbs 3:5-6, and talk with the children about how necessary it is that we pray for God's will to be done in our lives. God knows what is best for us, but we have to allow Him to bring it about. If we don't ask for God's will to be done, we tend to do things in our own way according to our own understanding. Encourage the children to ask God to give them understanding, to wait for Him to show His will, and to expect Him to keep His promise to listen.

# 47 ( Rx For Prayer )

OBJECTIVE: To use Scripture as a reminder of when and how to pray

*Appropriate for ages 9 to 12*

As a reminder to your students to pray daily, let them make "prescriptions" for prayer that they may take wherever they go.

Cut apart a sheet of poster board to make enough 3 by 5 inch rectangles for each student, or use index cards of the same size. Tell the children in your class to write "Rx For Prayer" at the tops of their cards. Beneath the title they should make seven vertical sections and write down at the top of each the seven days of the week. At the very bottom they will write, "Take one capsule each day."

For the "medicine," cut slips of paper about 1 by 2 inches long and have the students write a Scripture verse and prayer thought on each. Instruct the children to roll a piece of tape so that it can stick to both the card and the "prescriptions." Then the students should roll up the slips of paper and press them onto the pieces of tape. The "prescriptions" can be pulled off and read at any time.

Here are some suggested Scriptures and prayer thoughts:

a. I Samuel 12:23; Lord, help me to pray for others.
b. Psalm 61:1-2; Thank you, God, for hearing my prayers when I am troubled.
c. II Chronicles 7:14; Father, teach me to seek You humbly.

d. John 14:13-14; God, I thank You for Your promise to always answer my prayers.
e. Luke 11:11-13; You will always provide for my needs, Lord.
f. Proverbs 3:6; Help me, Lord, to acknowledge You and follow Your leading.
g. Psalm 102:17; I am grateful that the Lord hears my prayer.

# 48 Share-A-Need/ Share-A-Prayer

OBJECTIVE: To provide a simple way for students to share and pray for requests

*Appropriate for ages 6 to 9*

Sharing prayer requests during class time can be more meaningful for your students if the needs are prayed for on an individual basis. Instead of praying once for all the requests and praises given, allow the children to participate one-on-one in intercessory prayer for their classmates.

At prayer time, hand out slips of paper for the boys and girls to write out their prayer requests. Collect these slips in an offering plate, then pass the plate again. Each child who wishes to participate can take out a slip, pray for the request, and then take the slip home as a prayer reminder until the following week. Be sure to have follow-up on the requests and let the children share with the rest of the class when their prayers have been answered.

# 49 Prayer Charts

OBJECTIVE: To encourage the practice of praying daily

*Appropriate for ages 6 to 9*

Make a prayer chart for each child to take home for personal prayer use. Print PRAYER CHART at the top of a piece of paper. Under this heading print the days of the week, like a calendar. Ask the children to color in a star or to place a sticker in the box for each day of the week that they pray. Provide a new prayer chart for each new month.

Write the names of the members of your class on a poster for placement on the bulletin board. Place a gold star after the names of the boys and girls who prayed each day during the month. If you wish, keep track of the charts for an entire quarter.

# 50 | A Good Time To Pray

OBJECTIVE: To help children put their prayer thoughts into words

*Appropriate for age 8 to teens*

Write the following list where the children can see it clearly, such as on the chalkboard. Ask the boys and girls to choose one of the times when we should pray and to think of what someone might say to God at such a time. For instance, when we need God's guidance, we might pray, "Dear Lord, I don't know which choice to make. Help me to see Your will in this and to make the right decision."

Next give each student a sheet of paper and a pencil to write down his prayer thoughts. The length does not matter as long as the child feels free to express himself to God.

When the children are finished, mount their prayers on a bulletin board so that the other boys and girls can see what they have written.

We should pray when:
*   We are in trouble.
*   We feel happy.
*   We need forgiveness.
*   Others have a need.
*   We want help with something.
*   We worship.
*   We need God's guidance.
*   We are grateful.
*   Someone is sick.
*   We see nature's beauty.

# 51 Prayer Of Salvation

OBJECTIVE: To lead children in a prayer to accept Jesus as their Savior

*Appropriate for any age*

By the time you have used several of the projects in this book, the students in your class will be fairly well acclimated to the idea of prayer as conversation with God. They have learned about giving thanks, petitioning, interceding, and praising. They have been introduced to dozens of people in the Bible who prayed in a number of different situations. They have prayed formally and casually, for their family and for their church, in short sentences and in recitations.

These prayers are important, but none more so than the child's individual prayer for salvation.

He has heard of Jesus' love for him and naturally he believes that he loves the Lord. He needs to know, however, that he must accept Jesus as his own personal Savior and then grow in ways that are pleasing to Him.

Explain the plan of salvation to your class according to God's Word:

a. God loves us (I John 4:7-8).

b. We are separated from God's love because we all do wrong (Romans 3:23).

c. Even though sin brings death, God sent His Son to take the punishment for us (Romans 6:23, I John 4:9-10, I Peter 2:24).

[Here you may need to make it clear that the punishment Jesus took is not the reproof or correction given by parents and teachers. By dying on the cross, Jesus took the punishment which would have separated us from the presence of the Lord forever (II Thessalonians 1:9).]

d. To accept God's plan of salvation for us, we must pray, confessing our sins before God and asking Jesus to be our Savior (I John 1:9, Romans 10:9, Acts 16:31).

Some of the children may be ready to receive

Jesus. Any who clearly demonstrate concern for their wrongdoing and a desire to accept Christ should be given the opportunity to do so. On the other hand, do not force anyone to a premature decision.

Depending on the age group of your class, either lead the children in a prayer of salvation which they repeat after you, or allow time for the children to pray on their own.

Encourage those who have made a decision to tell others about it right away, thus publicly confirming the choice they have made.

Continue to pray for the children. Talk with each one individually, asking them to explain what they have done in receiving Jesus as their Savior. Listen carefully to discover their personal relationships with the Lord.

# 52 The Jericho Jog

OBJECTIVE: To learn through a physical activity to show concern for others

*Appropriate for ages 6 to 12 (and the entire congregation)*

You can involve your students in prayer for their friends and neighbors while also emphasizing the idea that we can pray anytime and anywhere.

The account of the Israelite conquest over Jericho is told in Joshua 6 — use it as a biblical example for the "Jericho Jog." Encourage the children in your class to jog around their neighborhood seven times, praying for the people who live there. Even if your students do not know their neighbors, the exercise will help the boys and girls to extend their circle of concern outside of their own families.

The "Jericho Jog" could also work well in conjunction with physical fitness or weight management programs involving adults from the congregation.

---

# Answers To Puzzles

Special Prayers Crossword
Page 18

Promise Word Search
Page 57

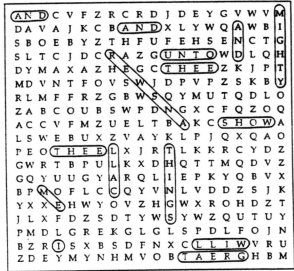